Spiders

Chris Graham

Rosen
REAL
READERS

Rosen Classroom Books and Materials
New York

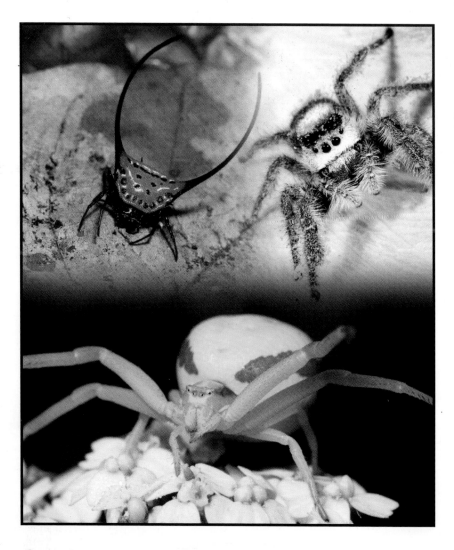

Spiders are small animals
with eight legs. Spiders come
in many different shapes and
colors.

Spiders live all over the world.
Some live on the top of cold
mountains. Others live under
the water!

Many spiders live in houses,
barns, and sheds. Look around
your house and you might
find one!

Spiders do not have bones.

Spiders are covered with a hard shell that keeps them safe.

Eyes

Most spiders have at least two
eyes. Some have four, six, or
eight eyes. Some spiders do not
have eyes at all!

Fangs

Spiders use two sharp **fangs** to catch and eat other animals. Some spiders use their fangs to dig nests in the ground.

All spiders make a sticky string
called **silk**. Spider silk is very
strong.

Most spiders make **webs** from silk. Spiders eat bugs that get trapped in their webs.

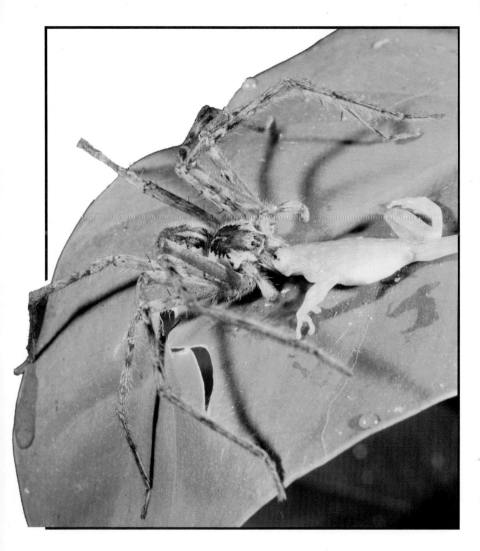

Some spiders do not use webs to catch their food. Some spiders **hunt** and eat bigger animals, like frogs, mice, and small fish.

Many spiders help people by catching and eating **pests**, like the bugs that eat our **crops** and bugs that can make us sick.

Glossary

crop   Plants grown by farmers for food.

fang   A long, pointed tooth.

hunt   To look for and kill animals for food.

pest   An animal that causes trouble for people.

silk   A thin, strong, sticky string made by spiders.

web   A net spiders make that is made of the silk from their bodies.